This book is dedicated

To my nephew Malachi,
and the graduating Class of 2025 —

As you enter this new season of life, my prayer is that this book equips you with wisdom, courage, and clarity to make sound decisions—financially, spiritually, and personally.

Malachi, may you lead with purpose and walk in the fullness of God's plan for your life. To every reader: may this be the beginning of breaking cycles, building legacy, and walking in Kingdom stewardship.

With love,
Keyonna Watton

Foreward

There's a major gap in today's culture: we teach young adults how to chase money, but not how to manage it. We tell them to dream big, but don't give them the tools to build. That's why this book matters — and why Keyonna Walton is the right voice to lead this conversation.

As a financial professional and founding member of The World Changers financial firm, I've helped people from all walks of life rewrite their financial story. But for me, this work is also deeply personal.

I grew up in a household where money was never talked about — at least not intentionally. We didn't discuss building wealth, investing, or stewardship. What we did hear was: get good grades, go to college, get a stable job, and do the "right" things. The message was well-meaning, but incomplete.

No one taught us how to build a budget, protect our credit, or create financial freedom. Like many others, I entered adulthood with ambition — but without strategy. And that's why I believe so strongly in what Keyonna has created here.

Make it Reign: A Financial Guide for Emerging Young Adults isn't just another workbook. It's a mindset shift. It's a blend of Kingdom truth and real-world financial strategy — presented in a way that's accessible, engaging, and empowering. Keyonna doesn't just teach finances — she teaches purpose. She doesn't just talk about money — she ministers to mindsets.

I've seen her work up close. Her expertise is solid, but what sets her apart is her heart. She's committed to breaking cycles and building legacies.

She's created something that every young adult needs —whether they're just starting their first job, heading to college, or navigating life's early decisions.

To every reader: this is your moment. You don't have to wait until you're older or wealthier or "more ready." Start now. This guide will walk with you, challenge you, and equip you to steward what's in your hands — and prepare for what's ahead.

Keyonna, thank you for being faithful to this assignment. I believe this book will impact thousands, and I'm honored to stand behind your work.

Let's build Kingdom wealth — on purpose, with purpose.

Daniel J. Thomas

Senior Executive Director, The World Changers

Table of Contents

01

Introduction

1.1 Welcome Letter 07
1.2 Looking Back 09
1.3 Different Set of Rules 11

02

Kingdom Wealth

2.1 Kingdom Wealth Journey 15
2.2 Cost of Poor Financial Decisions 21
2.3 Workbook Reflection 26
2.4 Kingdom Declarations 28

03

Money Mindset

3.1 Renewing Your Thinking 29
3.2 Workbook Activity 33
3.3 Breaking Generational Patterns 35
3.4 Prayer: Freedom & Renewal 38
3.5 Workbook Reflection 39
3.6 Mindset Declarations 40

04

Giving & Tithing

Why Give? 43
Everyone Tithes, But to Whom? 47
Offerings 49
Reflection Question 51
Prayer: For a Generous Heart 52
Workbook Prompt 55
Declaration: I Am a Good Steward 58

05

Budgeting & Planning Paycheck

4.1 Why Budgeting Matters 59
4.2 Creating Your First Budget 65
4.3 Planning Your Paycheck 69
4.4 Key Terms to Know 72
4.5 Kingdom Habits 76
4.6 Declarations: I Am a Planner 78

06

Savings

Why $1000 81
Closing Challenge: $1K Starter
Plan 89
Declarations: I Am a Saver 90

07

Building Credit

7.1 Credit 101 91
7.2 Key Terms to Know 97
7.3 Credit Score Breakdown 98
How to Use Credit Cards 99
Workbook Prompt 101
A Kingdom Mindset on Credit 105

08

Understanding Debt

What is Debt? 107
Types of Debt 115
Declarations: I Am Not a Slave
to Debt 116
Conclusion: You Are The 119
Change

WELCOME LETTER

Dear Graduate,

Congratulations! You're stepping into a brand-new season—a time filled with opportunities, decisions, and freedom. But with freedom comes responsibility. One of the most important areas you'll make decisions in is your money.

Whether you're working your first summer job or heading off to college with financial aid, scholarships, or a budget from your family, what you do with your money right now will shape your future. You are not just managing dollars—you are stewarding your future, your purpose, and your legacy.

This book was created to help you shift your mindset, build strong habits, and walk in the kind of wealth God intended—Kingdom Wealth. Not just for you, but for the generations that come after you.

Let's build wealth God's way—starting now.

With purpose,

Keyonna Watton
Financial Professional

Looking Back

Oh, what I would do to go back in time and apply what I know now! I can't say I had a clear game plan after high school, but in my mind, I just knew I'd be rich—and no one could tell me otherwise. I had big dreams of running businesses and owning multiple properties. I didn't know how I'd make it happen, but I was ambitious... and honestly, a little arrogant in my pursuit!

When it came to money, I didn't take heed to wise counsel. I started working my first official job at 16, but if you asked me where all that money went—I couldn't tell you. I didn't take saving seriously, and since I didn't have any real bills, I never learned how to truly budget or manage responsibilities. At the time, I thought that was a blessing. But looking back? Maybe it was more of a setup for the poor habits I carried into adulthood.

Fast forward to my twenties—I kept those same reckless spending habits. I still held onto this mindset that one day I'd be rich, so who cared if I was irresponsible or messed up my credit? I figured I'd fix it all later once I had money. Spoiler alert: that's not how it works. That mindset was broken. My relationship with money was toxic, to say the least.

But by God's grace, I've been through a transformational shift. It didn't happen overnight, but I've learned so many powerful lessons—lessons that cost me time, money, and peace.

I've done the hard mental and emotional work to break cycles and build a new foundation—so you don't have to repeat the same mistakes. And while I can't do the spiritual work for you, I can tell you this: your relationship with money is spiritual. Stewardship matters to God.

Which brings us to this book.

This isn't just a financial book. It's a mindset reset. It's a practical and spiritual guide to help you be a better steward over not just your finances—but over everything God has blessed you with.

If you have a desire to live a life of abundance and refuse to settle for a life of lack, this is for you. If you've watched your parents or loved ones struggle and feel a deep desire to break those cycles, this is definitely for you. And if someone handed you this book because they see your potential and want you to avoid the pitfalls they faced—this is especially for you.

So let's dive in. Your future self will thank you.

Living By a Different Set of Rules

Before we can talk about money, purpose, or stewardship, we have to first talk about the Kingdom. You may have heard that word before—maybe in church, maybe in prayer, maybe in a verse like "Seek first the Kingdom of God..." *But what does it actually mean?*

The Kingdom of God is not a place—it's a way of life. It's the rule and reign of God. It's a heavenly government with a King (Jesus), divine laws, principles, and culture that operate above and beyond the world's systems. When Jesus came to Earth, He didn't just come to save us from sin—He came to restore what was lost in the Garden of Eden: dominion, identity, and purpose.

When you live with a Kingdom mindset, you no longer measure your success by what the world celebrates—like fame, clout, or luxury. Instead, you learn to value things like wisdom, stewardship, obedience, peace, and legacy. The world teaches you to chase after money. **The Kingdom teaches you to master it and multiply it for a greater purpose.**

The World Teaches	The Kingdom Teaches
Get rich quick	Build wealth over time with wisdom
Flex now, worry later	Steward now, live in peace later
YOLO (you only live once)	Live with eternal purpose and generational vision
Chase the bag	Seek the Kingdom—everything else will be added
Do what feels good	Do what is right and righteous
You're on your own	You're part of a Kingdom family with divine backing

You see, when you align with the Kingdom, you gain access to divine strategy. God doesn't want you struggling, guessing, or hustling through life. He wants you to walk in purpose, with clarity, direction, and provision.

But the Kingdom requires participation.

Jesus said in Matthew 6:33, "Seek first the Kingdom of God and His righteousness, and all these things shall be added unto you." This means if you get your priorities right—putting God's way above your own desires—then everything else (money, housing, clothing, peace, opportunities) will follow.

This book is not just about how to budget or save better. It's about shifting your entire perspective. You were not born just to survive—you were born to reign. But reigning requires responsibility. And before God can trust you with more, He wants to see how you handle what you already have.

That's what Kingdom stewardship is all about.

So as we move forward, keep this in mind:

You're not just a young adult trying to figure life out. You're a Kingdom citizen with access to divine principles that can change your future—and your family's future—for good.

14

SECTION 2: YOUR KINGDOM WEALTH JOURNEY STARTS HERE

What is Kingdom Wealth?

Kingdom Wealth is more than money.

It is:
- Living in alignment with God's wisdom and provision
- Having more than enough to give, build, and grow
- Creating peace and legacy—not pressure and debt
- Becoming the one who breaks cycles, not repeats them

God doesn't just want you to "get by"—He wants you to walk in abundance, wisdom, and impact.

Kingdom Wealth

Imagine a life where you have more than enough, not only for yourself but also to help others. Kingdom Wealth encourages you to cultivate a generous spirit, where every act of giving is an investment in the future. It's about understanding that true wealth lies in relationships, purpose, and the positive change you bring to the world.

As you embark on your Kingdom Wealth journey, remember that it's a path of growth and transformation. It requires faith, dedication, and a commitment to stewarding your blessings wisely. This journey invites you to embrace opportunities to learn, to innovate, and to impact the lives of those around you.

In pursuing Kingdom Wealth, you're choosing a life of significance over mere success. It's about leaving a legacy of love, wisdom, and kindness, ensuring that those who follow can continue to build upon the foundation you've laid.

SCRIPTURAL FOUNDATION FOR THIS JOURNEY

"A good person leaves an inheritance for their children's children, but a sinner's wealth is stored up for the righteous."

— Proverbs 13:22

"Whoever can be trusted with very little can also be trusted with much, and whoever is dishonest with very little will also be dishonest with much."

— Luke 16:10

"But remember the Lord your God, for it is he who gives you the ability to produce wealth, and so confirms his covenant, which he swore to your ancestors, as it is today."

— Deuteronomy 8:18

The Power of Now: Why Early Financial Choices Matter

Let's take a moment to reflect on this, as you are either on the verge of starting to earn "your own" money or about to experience the reality of frugality as a college student. In either case, financial literacy will be crucial in helping you avoid repeating poor financial habits.

This isn't something you want to put off until you're 30 and in a huge amount of debt stuck working a job you hate, barely making ends meet.

The financial decisions you make today matter!

Studies show that 16% of young adults aged 18 to 24 already have debt in collections—meaning they're missing payments, damaging their credit, and setting themselves up for financial struggle early in life. It's not just about the numbers; it's about the weight of living paycheck to paycheck, the stress of avoiding phone calls from collectors, and the delay of dreams like owning a home or starting a family.

In fact, 74% of Gen Z borrowers have already delayed major life milestones because of debt. And perhaps most alarming, about one-third of young adults between the ages of 25 and 34 actually have negative wealth—meaning they owe more than they own.

But here's the good news: It doesn't have to be this way for you. Choosing to start saving now, being intentional with your money, and learning how to manage what you have can set you apart. Gen Z is already showing signs of breaking some of these patterns, with many beginning to save for retirement as early as 19 years old.

Even though only 16% of young adults report being fully financially independent today, those who develop financial discipline and responsibility early are the ones who walk into their 30s with freedom, options, and peace of mind.

This is about more than just money. This is about stewardship. It's about breaking generational patterns of lack, debt, and financial bondage. It's about building a new legacy rooted in wisdom, self-control, and a Kingdom mindset.

When you start now—whether by saving your first $1000, creating a simple budget, or learning how credit works—you're planting seeds that will produce an abundant harvest. Not just for you, but for your future family and the generations to come.

The power of now is real. Don't waste it.

The Cost of Poor Financial Decisions

You may think you're too young to start saving, building, or planning—but you're not.

- **Every smart financial choice you make today is a seed for your future.**

- **Every bad habit you refuse to carry forward breaks a chain in your family line.**

This isn't just about money—it's about your mindset, faith, and freedom.

It's about stewarding what God places in your hands with wisdom, not waste.

It's about choosing discipline over impulse so that the future version of you can walk in peace, not pressure.

And it's about stepping into adulthood knowing that you are not at the mercy of your circumstances—you've been given authority to change the narrative.

The earlier you start, the stronger your foundation will be. The decisions you make now will either set you up to struggle... or set you apart to thrive.

So don't wait. Start becoming who God called you to be—today.

"It won't matter right now" can turn into "I wish I had known" later.

Here are a few real-life examples to consider:

Example 1: The "I'll Just Pay the Minimum" Trap

Meet Maya:
Maya gets her first credit card at 19. She charges $1,500 for back-to-school shopping and some concert tickets, thinking, "I'll just pay the minimum—it's only $30 a month."

She ends up paying $2,300 over 5 years because of interest. Her credit score also drops because she kept her balance too high, making it harder to get approved for an apartment when she moved off campus.

Lesson: Credit cards aren't free money—and interest adds up fast. Paying the minimum may feel comfortable now, but it costs you so much more later.

Example 2: The "Keeping Up with the Joneses" Car Mistake

Meet Chris:

Chris just graduated high school and landed a summer job making decent money. Instead of saving or buying a reliable used car, he decides he wants to "pull up right" and get something flashy—a newer car with all the bells and whistles. Leather seats, sunroof, tinted windows. He's hoping it'll turn heads, especially on campus.

He takes out a loan with a $475 monthly payment, not realizing how quickly that eats into his checks. Within a few months, he's also spending hundreds more on premium gas, unexpected repairs, and expensive tires—because the nicer the car, the pricier the upkeep.

By the time school starts, Chris is stressed. He's working extra hours just to keep up with the payments. He can't afford books, has no money in savings, and barely has enough for gas and food. Worst of all? The car that was supposed to make him look successful is now keeping him broke.

Lesson: Buying things to impress people only leaves you stressed and struggling. Don't let pride or comparison drive your decisions. What's the point of having a "nice" car if you're broke behind the wheel?

Example 3: The "No Budget, No Boundaries" Trap

Meet Tiana:

Tiana landed a summer job and is making more money than she ever has before. Her checks are coming in fast, and with no major bills to worry about, she feels on top of the world. She goes out to eat almost daily, treats herself to new clothes, hits a few concerts with friends, and doesn't think twice about swiping her debit card.

Her mindset? "I'll start saving later—right now I'm just enjoying life."

She tells herself she'll budget next month... or the one after that.

But when school starts, reality hits—hard.

She needs to buy books, pay for a student parking pass, grab some essentials for her dorm, and now her job hours are cut because she's in class. She checks her account expecting a few hundred dollars. It says: $23.17.

She scrolls through her bank statement and can't even remember half the things she spent money on.

Now, Tiana's stressed, ashamed, and stuck. She's asking friends for gas money, skipping meals, and wishing she could go back and just plan a little better. She isn't lazy. She isn't dumb. She just didn't budget—and now she's paying the price.

Lesson: *Budgeting is not about being restricted—it's about being in control.*

Without a plan, your money will disappear without you even realizing it. A budget is a boundary that protects your future, not a punishment that limits your fun.

You don't rise to the level of your income—you fall to the level of your habits.

WORKBOOK REFLECTION

Money & You

1. What did you see growing up when it came to money? (Circle all that apply)
   - Struggle
   - Overspending
   - Stress
   - Saving
   - Giving
   - No conversation at all
   - Other: _ _ _ _ _ _ _ _ _ _ _

2. What is one bad money habit you want to leave behind?

3. What is one financial goal you'd like to reach this year?

MY COMMITMENT TO STEWARDSHIP

Take a moment to reflect and write your personal commitment to God as you begin this journey. This is not about being perfect—this is about being faithful.

Write your commitment statement below. Start with: "God, I commit to..."

God, I commit to...

_____

_____

_____

_____

_____

_____

_____

_____

(Sign & Date)

KINGDOM DECLARATIONS

- I am not a slave to money—I master it.

- I am the first in my family to save, sow, and steward well.

- I am faithful with the little, and God will trust me with more.

- I will break cycles and build a legacy through wise choices.

- God has given me the power to get wealth, and I will use it well.

- I have a Kingdom mindset and have authority over my finances.

SECTION 3: MINDSET SHIFT- RENEWING YOUR THINKING

"Do not conform to the pattern of this world, but be transformed by the renewing of your mind. Then you will be able to test and approve what God's will is—his good, pleasing and perfect will."

— Romans 12:2

LESSON 1: MONEY MINDSET MATTERS

Before we talk money, we have to deal with mindset.

What's a Money Mindset?

Your money mindset is the way you think, feel, and respond to money.

It comes from:
- What you heard growing up
- What you saw in your household
- What your environment taught you
- Your experiences with lack, struggle, or abundance

But here's the good news:
You can shift your mindset. You can unlearn fear, lack, and survival thinking and replace it with faith, wisdom, and Kingdom thinking.

Scarcity vs. Abundance

Scarcity Mindset		Abundance Mindset (Kingdom)
"There's never enough."	VS.	"God supplies all my needs."
"I have to hustle to survive."	VS.	"I steward well and trust God."
"Money is hard to come by."	VS.	"Wealth flows as I walk in purpose."
"I'll always be broke like my family."	VS.	"I'm breaking the cycle and building legacy."

Fill in the blanks with some of your own mindset shifts.

WORKBOOK ACTIVITY: Money Mindset Check

Circle the statements that reflect your current mindset:

- "Money stresses me out."
- "I believe God wants me to prosper."
- "I feel guilty when I have extra."
- "I've seen money cause problems in my family."
- "Saving money feels impossible."
- "I want to manage money in a way that honors God."

Now reflect:
Which mindset do you feel most pulled toward—scarcity or abundance? Why?

_____

_____

_____

_____

_____

LESSON 2: BREAKING GENERATIONAL PATTERNS

You are not just managing money for yourself. You're deciding what continues—and what stops—in your bloodline.

Common Patterns We Inherit:
- Living paycheck to paycheck
- Not talking about money
- Using credit cards to cover emergencies
- Spending to feel better
- No savings, no investments, no plan
- Refusing to tithe or give back

But you're different. You are called to break cycles.

Biblical Reminder

"Do not conform to the pattern of this world, but be transformed by the renewing of your mind. Then you will be able to test and approve what God's will is—his good, pleasing and perfect will."

– Romans 12:2

God isn't just calling you to be different. He's giving you the power to do it.

It Ends With Me!

When it comes to breaking generational patterns—especially around money—it starts with renewing your mind and applying the knowledge that God freely gives. The Bible reminds us in Hosea 4:6, "My people are destroyed for lack of knowledge." Think about that. Many of the people who suffer the most financially aren't lazy or incapable—they simply lack the wisdom and understanding of how to manage what they already have.

It's not always about needing more money. It's often about learning how to be a better manager of what's already in your hands.

There's a reason Proverbs 11:9 says, "Through knowledge shall the just be delivered." Deliverance—freedom from bondage—comes through learning and applying the truth. That includes financial freedom.

If you don't learn and grow, you risk repeating the same financial struggles you may have witnessed in your family. And sometimes, people reject knowledge not because it's unavailable, but because they're used to operating in ignorance.

But here's the good news: Jesus already broke the curse.

We talk about generational curses as if the blood of Jesus wasn't enough. As if His death and resurrection left us powerless. But that's a lie from the enemy.

The curse is already broken—you just have to walk in that freedom by changing the way you think, live, and steward what God gives you. The patterns of your bloodline don't have to define your future. You have the authority to say, "It ends with me."

This journey isn't just about money—it's about mindset, identity, and legacy. It's about becoming the one in your family who chose differently, thought differently, and lived differently—not by your own strength, but through Kingdom wisdom and the power of God.

Prayer: A Declaration of Freedom and Renewal

Father God,

Thank You for opening my eyes and giving me access to wisdom that leads to life. I confess that I have not always made the best choices or understood how to manage what You've placed in my hands. But today, I choose to walk in truth. I thank You that the curse has been broken through the blood of Jesus, and I no longer have to live under the weight of generational patterns that have kept my family bound.

Lord, renew my mind. Help me to see money, stewardship, and success through Your eyes. Uproot every lie I've believed about my worth, my future, and my limitations. Fill me with a desire to learn, to grow, and to honor You with every decision I make.

I declare that it ends with me. The cycle of lack, financial irresponsibility, fear, and ignorance is broken in Jesus' name. I receive Your wisdom, I receive Your grace, and I receive the calling to be a good steward—not just of money, but of the purpose You've placed in me.

Thank You for giving me the tools to succeed. May everything I learn from this day forward glorify You and transform my life and the lives of those who come after me.

In Jesus' name, amen.

WORKBOOK REFLECTION:
What's In My Hands?

1. What negative financial beliefs or patterns do you recognize in your family?

2. What habits do you want to break?

3. What legacy do you want to leave behind one day?

Mindset Declarations

Speak these over yourself regularly:

- I am not my past. I am God's promise.

- I am shifting my mindset and building new patterns.

- I walk in wisdom, faith, and financial favor.

- I don't follow the world's patterns—I follow God's purpose.

- I am the chain breaker in my family.

ACTIVITY: VISION SHIFT - From Survival to Stewardship

Write your response to each prompt below:

1. I used to think money was...

2. Now I believe money is a tool for...

3. One small step I can take this week to shift my money mindset is...

SECTION 4: Giving, Tithing & Generosity - The Kingdom Way

"Each of you should give what you have decided in your heart to give, not reluctantly or under compulsion, for God loves a cheerful giver."

— 2 Corinthians 9:7

WHY GIVE?

It's a way to partner with God in His work on earth.
- It reflects your faith that God will provide.
- It shows your heart toward others.
- It breaks the grip of greed and selfishness.
- It helps build kingdom wealth — wealth that blesses beyond yourself.

For many, the idea of giving money to the church feels uncomfortable—especially when you're young, don't earn much, or come from a background where money has always been tight. Maybe you've seen giving abused, or you've never really understood why God asks us to give in the first place. But when you see it through the lens of the Kingdom, tithing and giving are not about losing money—it's an act of worship, trust, and obedience.

What is tithing?

The word "tithe" means "tenth." Biblically, tithing is the act of returning 10% of your income back to God. But here's what we need to understand:
God isn't asking for your money—He's asking for a portion of what's already His.

Everything you have—your income, your opportunities, your gifts—comes from Him. Tithing is not a tax. It's not a religious fee. It's a faith-filled response of obedience, gratitude, and honor.

When we tithe, we're saying:
"God, I recognize that You are my Source. You gave me 100%, and I trust You enough to return 10% first—before anything else."

It's not about the amount. It's about the order and the heart behind it. Tithing teaches us to prioritize God, trust Him to provide, and break the grip of fear and greed that keeps us clutching what was never really ours to begin with.

"The earth is the Lord's, and everything in it..."
                                                            – Psalm 24:1

"Honor the Lord with your wealth, with the firstfruits of all your crops..."
                                                            – Proverbs 3:9

God could have asked for 90%, but He asks for just 10 —and blesses you for it. When you give to God first, you invite His wisdom and provision into the rest.

"Bring the whole tithe into the storehouse, that there may be food in my house. Test me in this," says the Lord Almighty, "and see if I will not throw open the floodgates of heaven and pour out so much blessing that there will not be room enough to store it."
                                                            — Malachi 3:10 (NIV)

This is one of the few times in Scripture where God says, "Test me." Why? Because He knows it takes faith to give away a portion of what you earn—especially when you feel like it's not enough to begin with. But God's economy doesn't work like the world's. When you give in obedience, you're not subtracting—you're sowing. And God promises a return.

EVERYONE TITHES—THE REAL QUESTION IS: TO WHOM?

Here's a hard truth we don't always think about:
Everyone is a tither.
The real question isn't "Will I give 10%?"—the question is "Where is my 10% going?"

Every week, we spend money—without hesitation—on what we value.

Whether it's entertainment, fast food, fashion, technology, or status symbols, we are constantly sowing into something.

For many, 10% or more of their income is already going to an idol—something they've elevated above God in their heart.

That might sound harsh, but it's worth reflecting on:
- Do I complain about tithing, yet give 10% or more to Starbucks, DoorDash, or concerts without thinking twice?
- Am I investing more in my image or my comfort than in God's Kingdom?
- Am I honoring the Creator of all things—or funding my own self-gratification?

When we cheat God of the tithe, we're not just withholding money—we're misplacing our worship.

Because money follows the heart, and your spending reveals what (or who) you truly trust.
"For where your treasure is, there your heart will be also."

– Matthew 6:21

God doesn't need your money—He wants your heart. And giving is one of the most honest reflections of where your heart is.

So before you say "I can't afford to tithe," ask yourself: Who or what is already getting your tithe—and are they worthy of it?

Only **_one_** gave you breath.
Only **_one_** formed you with purpose.
Only **_one_** provides in both seasons of plenty and seasons of lack.
Only **_one_** is worthy—and it's not Netflix or Nike.

Let your tithe reflect your faith, your trust, and your honor for the one and only true God.

WHAT'S THE PURPOSE OF THE TITHE?

- It teaches you to put God first (Deuteronomy 14:23)
- It supports the local church, its mission, and those in need
- It breaks the spirit of greed and fear
- It positions you for Kingdom blessing and provision
- It reminds you that everything you have is God's, and you're a steward, not an owner

What about offerings?

Offerings are above and beyond the 10%. These are the spontaneous, Spirit-led gifts you give—whether it's sowing into someone's life, contributing to a mission trip, or giving to a cause you believe in.

"Each of you should give what you have decided in your heart to give, not reluctantly or under compulsion, for God loves a cheerful giver."
— *2 Corinthians 9:7 (NIV)*

God doesn't want you to give out of guilt—He wants you to give out of joy, gratitude, and expectation. Giving is worship. It's a way of saying, "God, I trust You more than my paycheck."

Misconceptions About Tithing & Giving

- "The Church just wants my money."
👉 No, God wants your heart. But your heart and your money are deeply connected (Matthew 6:21).

- "I'll tithe once I make more money."
👉 If you don't learn to give from the little you have, you won't magically start when you have more. Start now. Build the habit.

- "I can't afford to give."
👉 Kingdom people believe, "I can't afford not to." Tithing isn't a burden—it's the key to breakthrough.

Giving as a Weapon in the Kingdom

- Giving isn't just financial—it's spiritual warfare. When you tithe and give, you:
- Declare that mammon (money) isn't your master
- Break the strongholds of poverty and scarcity in your bloodline
- Align yourself with divine order, where God is your Source

Want to break generational curses of lack? Start by aligning with Kingdom principles of generosity. You don't have to be rich to be a giver—you just have to be willing. Giving unlocks things in the spirit. It changes your mindset. It activates abundance. It protects your heart from greed and positions you to receive.

🛠️ Practical Tips to Start

1. Start where you are. Even if your paycheck is small, give your 10% faithfully and with a cheerful heart.
2. Be consistent. Don't just give when it feels good—make it a habit.
3. Track your giving. Watch what God does when you honor Him.
4. Pray over your seed. Speak life and purpose over every gift you give.

Tithing and giving are not about losing money. They're about walking in freedom, obedience, and purpose. When you trust God with your money, you'll find that He can do more with 90% than you ever could with 100%.

Reflection Question

"What is one mindset or fear I need to surrender in order to give the way God is calling me to give?"

_____

_____

_____

_____

_____

_____

_____

_____

_____

_____

_____

_____

A PRAYER FOR A GENEROUS HEART

Heavenly Father,

Thank You for being my Source, my Provider, and the Giver of every good and perfect gift. You have never withheld anything good from me, and I want to honor You with all that I have.

Lord, I admit there have been times I didn't fully understand tithing, giving, or why it even matters. But today, I ask for a heart of understanding. Open my eyes to see giving not as a loss, but as an act of faith, worship, and trust. Teach me to give cheerfully, not out of pressure, but out of love and gratitude for all You've done.

Create in me a heart that is free from fear, greed, or the desire to hold back. Teach me how to be a faithful steward of everything You've placed in my hands, whether it's a little or a lot. Help me to remember that all I have belongs to You, and that by giving, I'm sowing into something greater than myself—Your Kingdom.

Let my giving reflect Your generosity. Let it be led by Your Spirit and grounded in truth. Use what I give to impact lives, build Your church, and transform hearts. And may I never forget that I am blessed to be a blessing.

In Jesus' name,
Amen.

Journaling Prompt

Write about a time you struggled with the idea of giving—
whether it was giving your time, money, or energy. What was
going through your mind? How did it make you feel? Now
think about how God has always provided for you. What
would it look like to trust Him fully with what you have?

WORKBOOK PROMPT: My Giving Plan

I commit to giving _ _ _ _ _ _% of my income to God.

I will set aside giving money: ☐ Weekly ☐ Monthly
☐ Per paycheck

One cause or ministry I feel called to support:

_ _

DECLARATIONS: I AM A GENEROUS GIVER

- I trust God as my provider.

- I give with a joyful heart.

- My generosity breaks cycles of lack.

- I am a blessing to others.

- I build eternal wealth through giving.

BIBLICAL PERSPECTIVE ON PLANNING

*"Plans fail for lack of counsel, but with many advisers they succeed." – **Proverbs 15:22***

Planning is an exercise of faith. It's not about trying to control the future—it's about preparing in obedience and trusting that God will order your steps. Proverbs 15:22 says, "Plans fail for lack of counsel, but with many advisers they succeed." God honors preparation, especially when it's done with wisdom, accountability, and dependence on Him.

When you plan your finances, your time, and your decisions, you're showing God that you take stewardship seriously and that you're ready for more. Planning doesn't replace faith—it proves it. It says, "God, I trust You enough to prepare for what You're about to do."

ACTION STEPS THIS WEEK

1 Decide on your first giving amount and schedule

2 Research ways to give (church app, online, cash, envelopes)

3 Pray for a generous heart and wisdom to steward well

4 Share your giving goals with a trusted mentor or accountability partner

DECLARATIONS: I AM A GOOD STEWARD OF MY FINANCES

- I plan my spending and save for the future

- I make wise choices with my money

- I honor God with my financial decisions

- I am disciplined and focused

- I create space for blessings in my life

SECTION 5: BUDGETING & PLANNING YOUR PAYCHECK

"Suppose one of you wants to build a tower. Won't you first sit down and estimate the cost?"

— Luke 14:28

WHY BUDGETING MATTERS

A budget is not a restriction—it's a strategy.

It's how you tell your money where to go instead of wondering where it went.

Budgeting teaches:
- Responsibility – You're in charge of your money.
- Restraint – You learn to say no now to say yes later.
- Readiness – Life will hit... your budget makes sure it doesn't knock you out.

When you start budgeting now, you're preparing for:
- Unexpected expenses
- Real college costs
- Roommate issues
- Lifestyle temptations

WHY BUDGETING MATTERS

Budgeting is one of the most powerful tools you can use to take control of your financial future, yet it's something many people struggle with. In fact, research shows that about 25% of Americans don't maintain a monthly budget, and even among those who do, 84% admit to exceeding it at times. Shockingly, over half of Americans—around 55%—don't use a budget at all.

These numbers reveal a hard truth—many people are living paycheck to paycheck not because they don't make enough, but because they haven't learned how to manage what they have.

Why is budgeting such a struggle for so many? One major reason is the lack of financial education. Most people were never taught how to create or stick to a budget, and without that foundational knowledge, managing money can feel overwhelming and frustrating.

Add to that our culture of instant gratification and impulse spending—where it's easy to swipe a card or tap a phone and buy now without thinking about later—and it becomes clear how quickly a budget can fall apart.

For those with inconsistent or low income, budgeting feels even harder because it seems impossible to plan for expenses that fluctuate month to month.

Then there's emotional spending. Many people buy things when they're stressed, bored, or feeling down. These habits often start young and become deeply rooted, leading to poor financial decisions that are emotionally driven rather than value-based. Which can quickly derail even the best-laid plans.

Another reason is that many people set unrealistic budgets that don't reflect their actual needs or lifestyle. When a budget feels like punishment, it's only a matter of time before it's abandoned. Additionally, without tools or systems in place—like budgeting apps, envelope systems, or weekly check-ins—people may lack accountability and lose track of where their money is going.

And perhaps most importantly, many people have deep-rooted beliefs or habits about money shaped by their upbringing. If you grew up in a home where money was mishandled or scarce, it's easy to develop a mindset of fear, avoidance, or irresponsibility. Spiritually speaking, if you don't see yourself as a steward of what God has given you, you may lack the sense of purpose and responsibility that fuels intentional financial planning.

But here's the good news: Budgeting isn't about restriction—it's about alignment.

The Word of God reminds us that we are stewards —not owners—of what God entrusts to us. If you begin to see your money as a resource to manage wisely rather than just something to spend, your perspective will shift. Budgeting becomes a form of obedience, discipline, and preparation for the abundance God wants to release into your life.

You're not just creating a budget—you're creating a plan to walk in purpose, avoid unnecessary financial stress, and build a foundation for a life of abundance and stewardship. Stick with it. You have the power to be different, to do better, and to set a new standard for yourself and the generations after you.

You don't have to repeat the patterns of those who came before you. It ends with you.

CREATING YOUR FIRST BUDGET

Step 1: Know Your Income
Estimate what you'll make per month

→ $_ _ _ _ _ _ _ _ _ _ _ _ _

Step 2: List Your Expenses
- Transportation (gas, bus pass, etc.): $_ _ _ _ _ _ _ _
- Food & snacks: $_ _ _ _ _ _ _ _
- Personal care: $_ _ _ _ _ _ _ _
- Fun/entertainment: $_ _ _ _ _ _ _ _
- Giving (tithes/offerings): $_ _ _ _ _ _ _ _
- Savings: $_ _ _ _ _ _ _ _
- Other: _ _ _ _ _ _ _ _ _ _ _ _ _ _ _ _ _ _ $_ _ _ _ _ _ _ _

Step 3: Do the Math

Income − Expenses = $_ _ _ _ _ _ _ _ left over

→ Use leftovers to increase savings or giving, or plan for bigger goals.

THE 70/20/10 RULE

This breakdown is a powerful starting point:

Category	Percentage	Explanation
Spending	70%	For needs, bills, fun, gas, etc.
Saving	20%	For emergencies, future, big goals
Giving	10%	Tithing, offerings, generosity

THE 50/30/20 RULE

Category	Percentage	Explanation
Needs	50%	Rent, utilities, groceries, transportation, school supplies
Wants	30%	Eating out, entertainment, clothes, hobbies
Savings & Debt	20%	Emergency fund, savings goals, debt payments

THE 5-BUCKET BUDGET METHOD (For Students)

Category	Suggested %	Purpose
Tithe/Give	10%	Honor God **first** with what you receive
Save	10–30%	Pay yourself first – future emergencies, goals
Spend (Needs)	40–60%	Transportation, food, phone, books, etc.
Spend (Wants)	10–15%	Fun, eating out, entertainment
Invest/Learn	5–10%	Courses, books, conferences, growth

WORKBOOK PROMPT: Fill in Your Summer Budget Example

- Monthly income: $_____
- Tithe (10%): $_____
- Savings (20%): $_____
- Needs (50%): $_____
- Wants (15%): $_____
- Growth (5%): $_____

HOW TO ACTUALLY STICK TO IT

- Use a budgeting app: Try EveryDollar, YNAB (You Need A Budget), or Mint.
- Check in weekly: Look over your spending every Sunday night.
- Use cash for fun money: When it's gone, it's gone.
- Set mini goals: Save for something small first—a concert, a trip, a new laptop.

COLLEGE LIFESTYLE TRAPS TO AVOID

- Credit cards too soon – Don't use it for food, gas, or fun if you can't pay it off in full each month.
- Eating out constantly – Fast food adds up fast. Plan 3 meals/week out max.
- Emotional spending – Feeling stressed? Don't shop. Pray, pause, and plan instead.
- Living for the 'Gram – Don't go broke trying to look like you're rich.

Planning Your Paycheck

When planning your paycheck—especially stepping into your first job or managing summer income—it's crucial to be intentional. Your paycheck is a tool, not just a reward.

Here are some key things to consider when building a plan for every dollar:

1. Know Your Take-Home Pay (Net Income)

- Don't plan based on your hourly wage or salary alone. Understand how much actually hits your bank account after taxes, social security, and any deductions.
- Example: You may earn $15/hr, but only see ~$12.75/hr after taxes.

2. Create a Budget Before You Get Paid

- Give every dollar a job before you spend it.
- Use a budgeting method (like 70/20/10 or 50/30/20) to decide how much goes to:
  - Needs (transportation, food, phone, etc.)
  - Savings and giving
  - Fun money or wants (shopping, outings, etc.)

Planning ahead prevents impulse spending.

3. Pay Yourself First

- Build the habit of saving before spending.
- Set a goal like: "I'm saving $100 from each paycheck."
- Start building toward your first $1,000 emergency fund.
- Automate savings if possible to avoid temptation.

4. Prioritize Tithing & Generosity
- If you're following Kingdom principles, tithe 10% off your paycheck first.
- Giving first aligns your heart, puts God at the center, and helps break cycles of fear or greed.

5. Look Ahead—Not Just at the Week
- Don't just plan for this paycheck—think about the whole month or upcoming obligations (e.g., back-to-school needs, travel, birthdays).
- Avoid the "check-to-check" cycle by thinking long-term.

6. Track Your Spending
- Even a simple log (pen & paper or app) can show you where your money actually goes.
- You may find leaks—like $100/month on snacks, subscriptions, or impulse buys—that could go toward goals instead.

7. Adjust & Be Flexible
- Life changes—so should your budget.
- Don't beat yourself up if you mess up. Revisit and revise your plan regularly.
- The goal is progress, not perfection.

8. Set Boundaries & Avoid Lifestyle Creep
- Just because you're making money doesn't mean you need to spend more.
- Resist the urge to "flex" or keep up with friends. Protect your financial future by being disciplined now.

9. Remember the Bigger Picture

- Each paycheck is a building block toward financial freedom.
- Whether it's saving for school, a car, future travel, or just building good habits—your future self is counting on you.

REFLECTION: What Does Financial Peace Feel Like?

Check all that apply:

☐ Not needing to borrow from anyone
☐ Having money for both fun and future
☐ Not feeling anxious about bills or emergencies
☐ Feeling proud of yourself
☐ Honoring God with your finances
☐ Being the friend who can help, not just ask

Now write:

When I stick to my budget, I will feel

_____.

✨ **Affirmation:**

"I am a wise steward of everything God has given me. I plan with purpose, give with joy, save with discipline, and spend with discernment."

KEY TERMS TO KNOW

Earnings Section

Term	Definition
Gross Pay	The total amount you earned before any deductions (hourly rate × hours worked).
Net Pay	Your "take-home" pay — the amount you actually receive after taxes and deductions.
Hours Worked	The total number of hours you worked during the pay period.
Rate of Pay	How much you're paid per hour.
Overtime Pay	Extra pay for working more than 40 hours/week (usually 1.5x your regular pay).

KEY TERMS TO KNOW

Deductions (What's Taken Out)

Term	Definition
Federal Income Tax	Money taken out by the federal government based on how much you earn.
State Income Tax	Money taken by your state government (varies by state; not all have this).
Social Security (FICA)	Helps fund retirement benefits for others—and eventually for you.
Medicare	A federal health program you pay into for future medical coverage.
Other Deductions	This could include things like union dues, health insurance, or 401(k) contributions (if applicable).

KEY TERMS TO KNOW

YTD (Year-To-Date)

Term	Definition
YTD Gross	Total money you've earned so far this year before taxes.
YTD Net	Total take-home pay you've received so far this year.
YTD Deductions	Total amount taken out of your paychecks since the start of the year.

 Pro Tip:

Always compare **Gross Pay** vs **Net Pay** so you're not surprised when you see your direct deposit. Knowing what each deduction means helps you track where your money is going—and prepares you for filing taxes later.

Sample Pay Stub

ABC Company 51-2322286
123 Main Street,
Anytown, NY 10000.

Earnings Statement

Stub Number: **245**

Employee Info			SSN	Pay Schedule	Pay Period		Pay Date
John Smith (Emp.ID: STS001) 102 Main Street, Anytown, NY 10000.			XXX-XX-7889	Weekly	Feb 19, 2020 to Feb 25, 2020		Feb 26, 2020

Earnings	Rate	Hours	Total	YTD	Taxes / Deductions	Current	YTD
Regular Earnings	$10.00	40 hrs	$400.00	$400.00	Federal Withholding	$44.50	$400.50
					FICA - Social Security	$24.80	$223.20
					FICA - Medicare	$5.80	$52.20
					State Withholding	$20.00	$180.00
					Employer Taxes		
					FUTA	$24.80	$223.20
					SUTA	$44.50	$400.50

YTD Gross	YTD Taxes / Deductions	YTD Net Pay	Gross	Taxes / Deductions	Net Pay
$3,600.00	$855.90	$2,744.10	$495.00	$410.00	**$744.10**

What is your Gross Pay for this pay period?

What is your Net Pay (take-home pay)?

How many hours did you work?

Using the Net Pay from this paystub:

- How much would you give (10%)? $ _ _ _ _ _ _
- How much would you save (20%)? $ _ _ _ _ _ _
- What would you spend on needs? $ _ _ _ _ _ _
- What would you spend on wants? $ _ _ _ _ _ _

75

Kingdom Habits:
Faithfulness Starts With the Little

Truthfully—right now, it might not feel like you have much. Maybe your paychecks are small, your schedule is packed, or your college budget feels tight. But what if I told you this is exactly where you build the habits that determine your future?

In Luke 16:10, Jesus said, "Whoever is faithful with very little will also be faithful with much, and whoever is dishonest with very little will also be dishonest with much." This verse isn't just about money—it's a Kingdom principle. God isn't looking for how much you have; He's looking at how you handle what you've been given.

Many people wait until they're "making more" to start taking their finances seriously. They say, "I'll save later," or "I'll give when I have more." But the truth is, if you don't build good habits when you have little, you won't suddenly develop them when you have more. More money doesn't fix money problems—wisdom and stewardship do.

The Kingdom way is different. It's not about chasing riches—it's about managing what's in your hands with purpose, discipline, and faith. When you live by Kingdom habits, your money has a mission. Every dollar is a tool. Every decision is a seed. And when you honor God in the small things—like choosing to budget, save, give, and spend wisely—you're positioning yourself for greater responsibility and blessing.

Think about David in the Bible. Before he became king, he was faithful as a shepherd. He protected sheep, played his harp in secret, and honored God in private long before he was trusted with a throne. The same goes for you. The way you handle your finances now—your discipline, your heart, your mindset—is shaping the kind of future you're preparing to step into.

So start now. Start small. Pay attention to how you spend $20 just as seriously as you would $2,000. Practice generosity, budgeting, delayed gratification, and saving—even when it feels like a sacrifice. These aren't just financial habits; they're Kingdom habits. They reflect trust in God, self-control, wisdom, and a heart that's ready for increase.

The world says, "Live for the now." But the Kingdom says, "Live with purpose. Live for legacy."

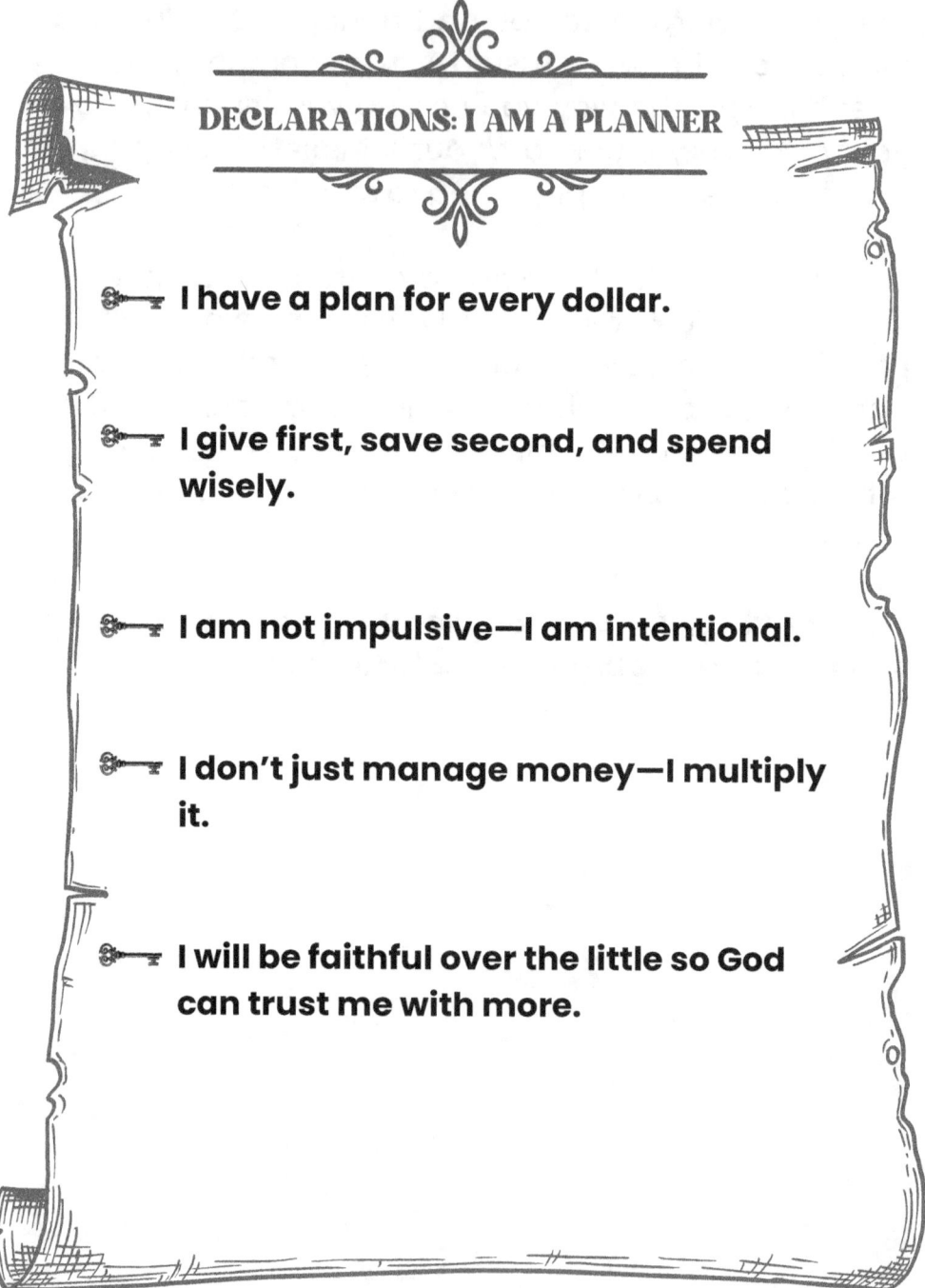

DECLARATIONS: I AM A PLANNER

🔑 I have a plan for every dollar.

🔑 I give first, save second, and spend wisely.

🔑 I am not impulsive—I am intentional.

🔑 I don't just manage money—I multiply it.

🔑 I will be faithful over the little so God can trust me with more.

ACTION STEPS THIS WEEK

1 Create your budget

2 Download a budgeting app

3 Set weekly budget check-ins

4 Tell someone you trust to help keep you accountable

ONE STEP at a TIME

SECTION 6: SAVING YOUR FIRST $1,000

"Go to the ant, you sluggard;
consider its ways and be wise!"
— Proverbs 6:6

WHY $1,000?

$1,000 may not seem like much—but for where you're starting, it's a powerful first goal.

This is not just about money—it's about discipline, decision-making, and direction. It's your first move from reacting to life... to preparing for it.

Your first $1,000 becomes:
- An emergency cushion
- Proof to yourself that you can do it
- The foundation for your financial future

This is your training ground.

Did You Know?
More than one in four Americans (28%) have less than $1,000 in savings. Among Gen Z, that number rises to 32%. This highlights how a lack of financial knowledge and planning can leave many vulnerable to emergencies and unexpected expenses.

This statistic underscores the importance of financial literacy and proactive money management. By educating yourself and making informed decisions, you can break free from this cycle and build a secure financial future.

THE 5-STEP PLAN TO SAVE YOUR FIRST $1,000

1. Set the Goal – Give It Purpose

Write this on a sticky note or lock screen:
"I will save $1,000 by [insert date]."

 Make it a SMART goal: Specific, Measurable, Achievable, Relevant, Time-based.

WORKBOOK PROMPT:
- My $1,000 savings deadline is:

  _ _ _ _ _ _ _ _ _ _ _ _ _ _ _ _ _ _
- Why I want to save this money:

  _

2. Open a High-Yield Savings Account

Use a separate account just for savings (not your checking account).

 Look for:
- No monthly fees
- Easy online access
- A high interest rate (3%–5%)
- Optional: banks like Chime, Capital One 360, Ally, SoFi or Vio Bank

Pro Tip: Don't get a debit card attached to this account. You'll be less tempted to dip into it.

THE 5-STEP PLAN TO SAVE YOUR FIRST $1,000

3. Create a Simple Savings Plan

Weekly Income	Amount to Save (10–30%)
$100	$10 – $30
$200	$20 – $60
$300	$30 – $90
$400	$40 – $120
$500	$50 – $150

Choose a percentage that works for your summer job or stipend and automate it. Set up auto-transfers to your savings weekly or biweekly.

WORKBOOK PROMPT:

- I will save $_ _ _ _ _ from each paycheck.
- I will automate my savings every:
  _ _ _ _ _ _ _ _ _ _ _ _ _ _ (day/date)

4. Track & Celebrate Progress

Use a tracker like the one below to watch your money grow. Color it in or check it off as you go!

$1,000 Savings Tracker:
[ ] $100
[ ] $200
[ ] $300
[ ] $400
[ ] $500 HALFWAY THERE
[ ] $600
[ ] $700
[ ] $800
[ ] $900
[ ] **$1,000**
  CONGRATULATIONS!!!
  KEEP GOING!!!

WORKBOOK PROMPT:

When I reach $1,000, I will celebrate by:

_____

5. Avoid the Trap of Spending It Too Soon

This is not shopping money. This is not "for later when I feel like I deserve a reward."

This is your seed. Your buffer. Your security.
Be faithful over it.

"The wise store up choice food and olive oil, but fools gulp theirs down." – Proverbs 21:20

BREAKING THE CYCLE: WHY THIS MATTERS

In many families, savings accounts didn't exist.
Emergencies became crises.
Broke became normal.
Debt became the default.

But when you save, you break those patterns:
- No more borrowing for every little problem
- No more asking everyone else to rescue you
- No more living check to check

You become the provider, the stabilizer, and eventually the wealth builder.

REFLECTION: WHAT IF YOU HADN'T SAVED?

Imagine your laptop breaks or you have an unexpected college cost.

Would you be:
- Calm and prepared?
- Stressed and scrambling?
- Asking friends/family for help again?

Now imagine you've got $1,000 saved.

You move differently. You think differently. You plan differently.

_____

_____

_____

_____

_____

_____

_____

CLOSING CHALLENGE: The $1K Starter Plan

Your mission this month:

- ☐ Open your savings account
- ☐ Set your goal and deadline
- ☐ Automate weekly savings
- ☐ Use the tracker
- ☐ Celebrate your first $1,000!

"Do not despise small beginnings..." – Zechariah 4:10

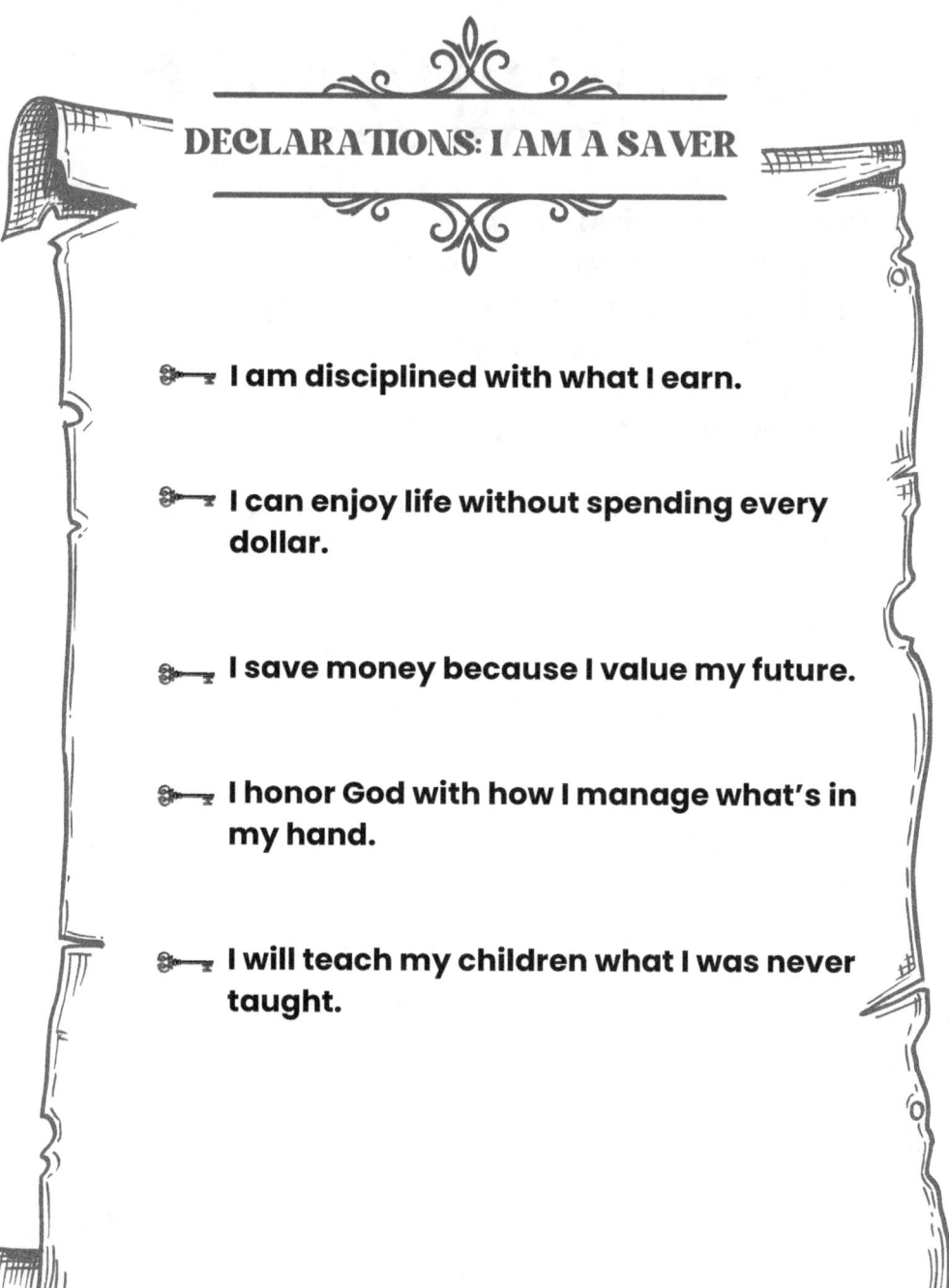

DECLARATIONS: I AM A SAVER

- I am disciplined with what I earn.

- I can enjoy life without spending every dollar.

- I save money because I value my future.

- I honor God with how I manage what's in my hand.

- I will teach my children what I was never taught.

SECTION 7: BUILDING CREDIT (THE RIGHT WAY)

"A good name is more desirable than great riches; to be esteemed is better than silver or gold."

— Proverbs 22:1

WHAT IS CREDIT AND WHY DOES IT MATTER?

Credit is your financial reputation.

It tells lenders, landlords, even future employers whether you're responsible or risky.

Your credit affects:
- Your ability to rent an apartment
- Getting a car or student loan
- Job applications (some employers check it!)
- Interest rates (how much extra you pay to borrow money)

Good credit = lower stress, more freedom.
Bad credit = higher costs, more limitations.

Credit 101: Build It Right the First Time

Let's talk about something most people wish they would've understood sooner: credit.

Credit is like a financial reputation. It's a score that tells lenders, landlords, and sometimes even employers whether or not you're trustworthy with money. Sounds simple, but here's the catch: your credit can either set you up for success or silently sabotage your future. And you don't get to start over just because you didn't know.

Many young adults mess up their credit early—maxing out credit cards, missing payments, co-signing loans they can't afford—thinking, "I'll fix it later." But here's the truth: bad credit takes seconds to mess up and years to rebuild. One missed payment can stay on your report for up to seven years. Seven.

So what is credit and why does it matter?

Your credit score is a three-digit number (usually between 300 and 850) that measures how well you manage borrowed money. Your score is used to determine things like:
- Whether you get approved for a car loan, apartment, or mortgage
- What interest rate you'll pay (higher score = lower rate = less money wasted)
- Whether you get certain jobs or access to utilities without deposits

So imagine this: Two people apply for the same car. One has a credit score of 750, the other 580. The person with good credit may pay hundreds less per month just because they were wise and responsible early on. That's the power of credit.

How do you build good credit?

1. **Start small and smart** – Consider a student-friendly credit card or secured credit card with a low limit. Use it only for small, planned purchases (like gas or groceries), then pay it off in full every month.
2. **Pay on time—every time** – Your payment history is the biggest factor in your score. Set up automatic payments or reminders.
3. **Keep your balances low** – Try not to use more than 30% of your available credit. (So if your limit is $300, don't carry a balance over $90.)
4. **Don't open too many accounts at once** – Every time you apply for credit, it's a hard inquiry. Too many at once can hurt your score.
5. **Don't co-sign for friends or family** – It may seem kind, but their financial habits will directly impact your credit score. Protect your future.

Why does this matter now?
Because time is your greatest asset. The earlier you start building good credit, the better off you'll be when it's time to get a car, rent your own place, or buy a home. Good credit opens doors. Bad credit builds walls. And choosing to ignore your credit score doesn't make it go away—it just gives it power over you.

From a Kingdom perspective, your credit is a reflection of stewardship. It's not about chasing material things—it's about being trustworthy. Scripture says in Luke 19:17, "You have been faithful with a little; now you will be trusted with more." If you learn to manage even small amounts of money and credit well now, you're preparing for greater blessings later.

HOW TO START BUILDING CREDIT (THE WISE WAY)

1. **Get a Starter Credit Card**
   - Look for: student credit cards or secured credit cards
   - Only use it for small fixed costs (like a monthly subscription or gas)
   - Pay it off in full every month – not just the minimum!
2. **Make On-Time Payments a Habit**
   - Set up auto-pay or calendar reminders
   - Even one late payment can hurt your score for years
3. **Keep Utilization Low**
   - Only use 10-30% of your available credit
   - (If you have a $500 limit, try not to charge more than $150 monthly)
4. **Don't Open Too Many Accounts**
   - Each time you apply for credit, it lowers your score slightly
   - Be patient—building credit is a marathon, not a sprint

KEY TERMS TO KNOW

Term	Definition
Credit Score	A number (300–850) that shows how reliable you are with money
Utilization Ratio	The % of your credit limit you're using—lower is better
Interest Rate (APR)	The cost of borrowing if you don't pay off the balance
Secured Credit Card	Requires a deposit; great for beginners
Credit Report	A summary of your credit history (check free yearly at AnnualCreditReport.com)

COMMON CREDIT TRAPS TO AVOID

▶ Using credit for things you can't afford
▶ Carrying a balance and paying interest
▶ Missing payments or forgetting due dates
▶ Co-signing for friends or family
▶ Letting debt pile up "just a little at a time"

Remember: Credit is a tool, not a treat. Use it with self-control, not emotion.

CREDITSCORE BREAKDOWN

Payment history	35% ✅ Pay on time, every time
Amount owed (utilization)	30% ✅ Keep balances low
Length of credit history	15% ✅ Keep old accounts open
New credit inquiries	10% ✅ Avoid too many new cards
Types of credit used	10% ✅ Mix of loans/cards helps

Score ranges:
- 800–850: Excellent
- 740–799: Very Good
- 670–739: Good
- 580–669: Fair
- Below 580: Poor

Credit Cards: How to Use Them Wisely, Not Recklessly

A credit card can either be a tool or a trap—and the difference lies in understanding how it works.

✨ Credit Card Basics:

- **Credit Limit:** The max amount you're allowed to borrow on your card.
- **Minimum Payment:** The smallest amount you can pay by the due date to avoid late fees. (Hint: Paying only this keeps you in debt longer!)
- **APR (Annual Percentage Rate):** The yearly interest rate you're charged on balances you carry. Some cards have 20% APR or higher—that means if you carry a balance, you're paying way more than what you spent.
- **Due Date:** The date by which you must make a payment to avoid penalties.
- **Grace Period:** The window (usually 21–25 days) after your purchase when you can pay your balance in full without being charged interest.

Principle vs. Interest

- **Principal:** The original amount you borrowed or charged.
- **Interest:** The cost of borrowing the money—charged when you don't pay the full balance by the due date.

If you only pay the minimum payment, most of that goes toward interest—not the principal. So your debt barely moves while your interest keeps growing.

Strategy: How to Use a Credit Card Without Falling Into Debt

1. Only charge what you can pay off in full
Treat your credit card like a debit card. If you don't have the money in the bank, don't swipe it.

2. Pay off the full balance every month
This avoids interest charges completely. It's the smartest way to build credit while staying debt-free.

3. Pay early (or twice a month)
This lowers your credit utilization (how much credit you're using), which helps boost your score.

4. Understand your APR
If you do carry a balance, know how much interest you're paying. You'll quickly see why it's best to pay in full.

5. Avoid late payments at all costs
One missed payment can drop your credit score by 50–100 points and stay on your report for 7 years.

Real Example:
You spend $500 on a credit card with 22% APR and only pay the $25 minimum each month.

It will take 2.5 years to pay it off, and you'll end up paying over $650 total. That's $150+ in interest—for a $500 purchase!

Bottom Line:
"Credit isn't free money. It's borrowed money—with a price tag."

Use credit as a tool to build your score, not as a crutch to fund a lifestyle you can't afford.

WORKBOOK PROMPT: Build Your Credit Plan

Do I already have a credit card? YES / NO

What will I use it for (only one or two expenses)?

→ _____

My repayment method (e.g., auto-pay, calendar alerts):

→ _____

My credit goal for 1 year:

→ _____

Credit Card Strategy Worksheet

Step 1: Know What to Look For

Review the sample credit card statement below and use the questions that follow to train your eye and mind for real-world use.

Sample Credit Card Statement

Name: Jordan Smith

Credit Card Issuer: Growth Bank

Statement Period: July 1 – July 31

Credit Limit: $1,000

Previous Balance: $320.00

New Charges: $150.00

Payments Made: $50.00

Interest Charged (APR: 21.99%): $6.29

New Balance: $426.29

Minimum Payment Due: $30.00

Due Date: August 15

Step 2: Think It Through – Answer the Questions

What is Jordan's current balance?

How much has Jordan been charged in interest this month?

If Jordan only pays the minimum ($30), what happens to the remaining balance next month?

What's one financial risk of continuing to carry a balance on this card?

How could Jordan avoid interest charges altogether next month?

What percentage of their credit limit is Jordan currently using? (Hint: Balance ÷ Credit Limit)

Is this usage good or bad for their credit score? Why?

If Jordan's goal is to pay off the full balance in 2 months, how much should they pay each month?

A KINGDOM MINDSET ON CREDIT

"The rich rule over the poor, and the borrower is slave to the lender." – Proverbs 22:7

- We don't worship credit—we master it.
- We don't chase debt—we steward opportunity.
- Our goal is not to "buy now, pay later"—but to own now, honor always.

Good credit is not just about access—it's about trust.

It shows you can be trusted with what's borrowed, which reflects how God can trust you with more.

DECLARATIONS: I AM RESPONSIBLE

🗝 I use credit to build, not to burden.

🗝 I pay what I owe, on time, every time.

🗝 I avoid impulse and choose wisdom.

🗝 I am building a solid financial foundation.

🗝 I will be debt-free and credit-strong, in Jesus' name.

ACTION STEPS THIS WEEK

1 Research 1-2 student credit card options

2 Talk to a parent/mentor before applying

3 Write down how you'll use your credit card wisely

4 Sign up for Credit Karma or Experian to monitor your score

5 Learn how to request your free credit report at AnnualCreditReport.com

SECTION 8:
Understanding Debt
& How to Avoid It

"Let no debt remain outstanding, except the continuing debt to love one another, for whoever loves others has fulfilled the law."

— Romans 13:8

WHAT IS DEBT?

Debt is money you borrow that you are required to pay back—usually with interest (an extra cost).

Types of common debt for young adults:
- Credit cards
- Student loans
- Car loans
- Personal loans
- Buy Now, Pay Later programs (Klarna, Afterpay, etc.)

Debt isn't just a number—it's a weight. The more you owe, the less freedom you have.

THE CONSEQUENCES OF DEBT

Consequence	Why It Matters
Interest Adds Up	You end up paying way more than you borrowed
It Limits Your Options	Debt payments reduce how much of your money you actually keep
It Delays Your Future	Can't save, invest, or grow because you're paying the past
It Causes Stress & Shame	Many young adults suffer mentally and emotionally because of debt

The Dangers of Debt

In a world that normalizes debt, credit card balances, student loans, car payments, and "buy now, pay later" options, it's easy to believe that debt is just a part of life. It's one of the biggest traps young adults walk into— sometimes unknowingly, often thinking it's "normal." **But just because something is common doesn't make it Kingdom.**

Why is debt dangerous?

When you're in debt, you're not in control—your paycheck belongs to someone else before it even hits your account. Debt limits your options, delays your goals, and causes stress, strain, and anxiety. And beyond the financial impact, it affects your ability to be a cheerful giver, to invest in your future, or to respond freely when God tells you to move or give.

📖 What does the Bible say about debt?

"Give to everyone what you owe them: If you owe taxes, pay taxes; if revenue, then revenue; if respect, then respect; if honor, then honor. Let no debt remain outstanding, except the continuing debt to love one another, for whoever loves others has fulfilled the law."
— *Romans 13:7-8 (NIV)*

This verse teaches us a Kingdom principle: the only thing we should owe is love—not loans, not overdue bills, not credit card debt. When you're bound by debt, it's harder to focus on generosity, calling, and community. You begin making decisions based on survival, not purpose.

"The rich rule over the poor, and the borrower is slave to the lender."

— Proverbs 22:7 (NIV)

Let that settle. Debt is slavery. That new phone, outfit, or car might feel good in the moment, but if it's borrowed on credit you can't repay, you've traded freedom for a temporary feeling. It's not just about what you're buying —it's about who ends up owning your time and money.

"Do not be one who shakes hands in pledge or puts up security for debts; if you lack the means to pay, your very bed will be snatched from under you."

— Proverbs 22:26-27 (NIV)

This paints a clear picture: debt doesn't just affect your wallet—it puts your stability at risk. In today's terms, debt can get your car repossessed, your account garnished, or your credit ruined—forcing you to live in financial stress and scarcity.

"The wicked borrow and do not repay, but the righteous give generously;"

— Psalm 37:21 (NIV)

This verse reminds us that paying back what we owe is not just financial—it's moral and spiritual. Avoiding debt, or at the very least repaying it with integrity, reflects righteousness and maturity in Christ.

How does debt show up early?

- Opening credit cards with no plan to pay them off
- Taking out student loans without understanding the repayment terms
- Financing things you can't truly afford to impress others
- Falling for "buy now, pay later" offers with hidden fees or high interest
- Ignoring the habit of budgeting and overspending month after month

What starts as "just a small monthly payment" can quickly become a mountain of financial weight that follows you for years.

So why is debt so dangerous, especially for young adults?

- It destroys your credit before you've even had a chance to build it.
- It delays major life milestones like buying a home, starting a business, or even getting married.
- It steals your peace, causing anxiety and stress you don't need while trying to grow and become.
- It teaches the wrong habits—that it's okay to live beyond your means.
- It ties your hands, keeping you from giving, tithing, investing, or serving freely.

And here's the kicker: most debt isn't accumulated out of necessity—it's a result of poor planning, lack of discipline, and emotional or impulse spending.

You don't have to live in debt.

You don't have to follow the patterns of culture or even the financial habits you may have seen growing up. You can break the cycle. You can make the decision now, before life really starts to happen, that you will walk in wisdom, freedom, and financial peace.

This isn't about perfection—it's about intentionality. If you've already made some money mistakes or taken on debt, don't feel condemned. That's not what God wants. Instead, receive the truth and make the decision to turn it around—to seek knowledge, ask for guidance, and steward what you have with integrity.

Kingdom Perspective: Debt-Free = Purpose-Filled

God did not create you to live under financial pressure or enslavement. He wants you to be a lender, not a borrower (Deuteronomy 28:12). He wants you to walk in freedom, purpose, and provision—not paycheck to paycheck.

This doesn't mean you can never take on a student loan or a mortgage wisely, but it does mean you need to learn to discern the difference between wise investment and wasteful bondage.

🛠️ What Can You Do Now?
- Start living on a realistic budget.
- Only borrow what you need, and have a clear plan to repay it.
- Avoid "buy now, pay later" schemes and high-interest credit cards.
- Pay everything on time—even the small bills.
- Ask God to help you shift from a mindset of lack to a lifestyle of stewardship.

Debt is not just a money issue—it's a mindset issue. And Kingdom people don't live bound. You were created to walk in freedom. And it starts with how you handle what's in your hands.

STUDENT LOANS

If you must take out student loans:
- Borrow the least amount possible
- Apply for grants, scholarships, and work-study first
- Understand what you're signing—read the terms!
- Start thinking now about how you'll repay it

"Just because they offer it doesn't mean you need it." Be prayerful before signing anything.

STRATEGIES TO AVOID DEBT

Create a real budget (not just in your head)
- Build a solid savings for emergencies

Live within your means
- Just because you can afford it, doesn't mean you should buy it.
- Stick to your budget. Delay gratification.

Use Credit for Purpose, Not Pleasure
- Credit cards are not "free money." They're tools.
- Use for emergencies or regular, planned expenses only.

Avoid impulse spending
- Be content—it's okay not to have what everyone else does
- Pay in full or wait until you can

God wants you to be a lender, not a borrower (Deuteronomy 28:12).
That starts with avoiding unnecessary debt—and wisely managing the debt you do have.

TYPES OF DEBT: KNOW THE DIFFERENCE

Type of Debt	Description	Wisdom Tip
Credit Card	High interest, revolving credit	Pay in full monthly or below 30% utilization.
Student Loans	Funds for education	Borrow only what's needed & apply for grants.
Car Loans	For buying a vehicle	Buy used, put down a large deposit
Personal Loans	Borrowed lump sums	Avoid unless absolutely necessary
Buy Now Pay Later	Delayed payments (Klarna, AfterPay)	Easy trap—use with extreme caution

DECLARATIONS: I AM NOT A SLAVE TO DEBT

 I break every generational curse of debt, poverty, and overspending.

I choose wisdom, not waste.

I have what I need; I will wait for what I want.

I am a lender, not a borrower.

My future will not be burdened by poor decisions—I walk in financial freedom.

WORKBOOK PROMPT: My Boundaries with Debt

What kind of debt do I want to completely avoid?

How will I keep myself from impulse spending?

What's one money habit I will commit to now to protect my future?

ACTION STEPS THIS WEEK

1 Look at a breakdown of how interest works (try a debt calculator online)

2 Talk to a trusted adult or financial advisor before signing any loan documents

3 Write out your "Debt-Free Vision" — what your life will look like without the weight of debt

4 Commit to your "Avoid Debt" plan and stick to it this summer

Conclusion: You Are the Change

You've made it to the end of this book—but this isn't the end of your journey. It's the beginning of a new mindset, a new standard, and a new legacy.

You've learned that financial wisdom isn't just about numbers—it's about obedience, discipline, and identity. It's about knowing that you were never meant to live in cycles of survival, debt, or lack. You were created to walk in freedom, to build, and to leave something better behind for those who come after you.

God has entrusted you with time, talents, resources, and influence. This is your moment to break generational patterns and start living with intentionality. You now understand what it means to be a Kingdom steward—faithful over the little, so God can trust you with more.

Don't despise small beginnings. Don't let fear or comparison cause you to delay your progress. And don't wait until life forces you to care—choose now to be different.

Proverbs 21:5 says, *"The plans of the diligent lead surely to abundance, but everyone who is hasty comes only to poverty."*

So be diligent. Be faithful. Be wise.

Make the budget.
Write the vision.
Ask the hard questions.
Tell your money where to go.
Return the tithe with joy.

Invest in your future—spiritually and financially.
You don't have to be perfect. You just have to be committed.

Because when you change your mind, you change your habits.

When you change your habits, you change your future.
And when you change your future—you change your family line.

You are the repairer of the breach.
You are the curse breaker.
You are the good steward.
So go be faithful.
Go be free.
And go be who God created you to be.

CHATGPT FINANCIAL PROMPTS

50 Smart Prompts to Strengthen Your Finances
Use these questions to get practical, personalized advice from ChatGPT. Think of it like having a virtual financial advisor on call—anytime you need clarity or a game plan.

Budgeting & Planning

1. Help me create a realistic budget as a college student with a part-time job.
2. How can I start a zero-based budget with irregular income?
3. What are common budgeting mistakes young adults make—and how can I avoid them?
4. Help me set up a simple 70/20/10 or 50/30/20 budget based on $500/month income.
5. How can I track my spending when I mostly use a debit card and cash?
6. How much should I have in an emergency fund if I make $1,200/month?
7. I just got my first job—how should I plan my paycheck?
8. Help me figure out a budgeting system that keeps me consistent and motivated.

Saving & Cash Flow

1. Help me create a savings plan to reach $1,000 in 90 days.
2. I want to start saving but my income is low—what should I do first?
3. What are smart ways to automate savings without feeling broke?
4. What are high-yield savings accounts that are good for young adults?
5. What are 10 things I should stop spending on if I want to save more?

Income Building

1. What are part-time jobs or side hustles for students that pay well?
2. Help me brainstorm ways to monetize my skills or hobbies.
3. How do I start freelancing online as a beginner?
4. What income streams can I build before I turn 25?
5. I want to earn extra money without getting another job—what are my options?

Credit & Credit Cards

1. What's the best beginner credit card for a college student?
2. Help me understand how APR works and how to avoid paying interest.
3. What's credit utilization and how does it affect my score?
4. How do I check my credit score for free and monitor it monthly?
5. Should I pay off my credit card in full every month or carry a balance?
6. I want to build credit without going into debt—what are my options?
7. I'm trying to build a credit score from scratch. Can you create a 6-month credit-building game plan?

Debt & Loans

1. How do I know if a loan or payment plan is a bad idea?
2. Show me how long it would take to pay off $1,000 of credit card debt with $50/month payments.
3. I'm thinking about taking out student loans—what should I know first?
4. How do I avoid payday loans or fast cash traps?
5. What's a good strategy to pay off debt while still saving?

Investing & Long-Term Thinking

1. How do I start investing if I'm brand new and only have $100?
2. What is compound interest and how can I make it work for me early?
3. Should I invest or save first if my income is limited?
4. Explain the difference between a Roth IRA and traditional IRA in simple terms.
5. What is a mutual fund vs ETF? Which is better for beginners?

Paychecks & Taxes

1. Help me understand my paystub—what do all the deductions mean?
2. What's the difference between gross income and net income?
3. What apps or tools help young adults file taxes for free?
4. I'm starting a job—how do I fill out my W-4 correctly?

Smart Data-Based Prompts

1. Upload a recent bank or credit card statement and ChatGPT will identify recurring subscriptions and recommend which ones to cancel or downgrade.
2. These are the last 10 purchases on my debit card—can you categorize them into needs vs. wants?
3. Here's how much I earned and my bills this month. Can you create a budget and savings plan for me?
4. Here's my credit card balance, due date, and APR. What's the smartest payment strategy this month?
5. Compare my current checking account with other high-yield savings or student-friendly banks—what should I switch to?

🛠 Tools, Evaluations & Scenarios

1. Compare my current checking account with other high-yield savings or student-friendly banks—what should I switch to?
2. These are my side hustle ideas. Based on market trends and my skills, which one should I prioritize?
3. Here's a job I'm considering. Based on the hourly pay and estimated taxes, how much will I actually take home each month?
4. These are my current monthly expenses. Can you show me how to create sinking funds for school, travel, or emergencies?
5. I'm trying to build a credit score from scratch. Can you create a 6-month credit-building game plan?
6. What percentage of my paycheck should go toward savings, bills, giving, and fun?
7. How can I build a monthly financial routine to stay on track?

A Word of Wisdom: AI Is a Tool, Not the Source

As helpful and powerful as AI tools like ChatGPT can be, they are just that—tools. Artificial intelligence is not all-knowing, all-wise, or all-powerful. It is not your Savior, your Counselor, or your Source of Truth. The wisdom that truly transforms lives comes from God alone, through His Word and the Holy Spirit.

Always remember:
"But the Advocate, the Holy Spirit, whom the Father will send in my name, will teach you all things..." – John 14:26

Before making any financial decisions, pray. Ask God for discernment and clarity. The Holy Spirit gives supernatural wisdom that no algorithm can replicate. AI may be able to analyze numbers—but only God can align your heart, mind, and purpose.

📌 And while AI can give you suggestions, real financial advice should come from real people with real experience and credentials—licensed financial advisors, certified accountants, trusted mentors, and Kingdom-minded professionals.

So, use this technology as a support system—not your source.

Let it assist you—not lead you.
Let the Holy Spirit always be your guide—in finances and in life.

Ready to Keep Growing?

Don't let your financial journey stop here.

Get access to exclusive resources, tools, and bonus training to help you build wealth, walk in wisdom, and live with purpose.

- Download free printable budgeting tools & digital products
- Get our curated list of recommended banks, apps & books
- Use bonus ChatGPT prompts to analyze your finances
- Join the Make it Reign email list for updates, tips, and mentorship opportunities
- Be the first to know about live workshops, Q&A sessions, and future releases!

Scan the QR Code below to access your free resources You've started the journey. Let's walk it out together.